Viewing the Guru Through the Lens of the Seven Limb Puja

Viewing the Guru Through the Lens of the Seven Limb Puja

This is a Dharma teaching from
Jetsunma Ahkön Norbu Lhamo at Kunzang Palyul Chöling
on October 18, 1995. It is one of a series of teachings given
by Jetsunma during a retreat that focused on devotion
and the proper way of viewing one's Guru.

Wild Dakini LLC
P.O. Box 304
Poolesville, Maryland 20837 USA
www.wilddakini.com

Copyright © Jetsunma Ahkön Norbu Lhamo 2016

All rights reserved. No part of this book may be reproduced in any form electronic or otherwise, without written permission from Jetsunma Ahkön Norbu Lhamo.

Printed in USA.

ISBN 978-0-9855245-3-1
1. Spirituality 2. Buddhism

Library of Congress Control Number 2016962074

Viewing the Guru Through the Lens of the Seven Limb Puja / by Jetsunma Ahkön Norbu Lhamo

Cover Art: Thangka Painting of Padmasambhava and his Indian consort, the Princess Mandarava by Soyolmaa Davaakhuu

Contents

Introduction vii
Viewing the Guru Through the Lens of the Seven Limb Puja 1
    What Do We Offer the Guru? 13
        Offering the Cup of Hatred 13
        Offering the Cup of Greed and Grasping 13
        Offering the Cup of Ignorance 14
        Offering the Cup of Jealousy 15
        Offering the Cup of Pride 16
        Turning Away from the Guru 19
    Applying the Seven Limb Puja 23
        Paying Homage 23
        Making Offerings 27
        Confession 31
        Rejoicing 33
        Requesting Teachings 37
        Beseeching the Buddhas, Bodhisattvas,
            and Lamas to Remain 43
        Dedication 49
The Seven Limb Puja (English and Tibetan) 55
Glossary 63
Dedication 67
About Jetsunma Ahkön Lhamo 69

Introduction

Lord Buddha Shakyamuni practiced the Path for three countless aeons before he attained complete enlightenment. We can read in the Jataka Tales stories of the Buddha's past lives, about his challenges and his accomplishments. Even if we are certain of the truth of the stories and inspired by the Buddha's accomplishment, how can we, who are only ordinary beings, possibly do what the Buddha did? The sutras tell us about his lack of fear, his certainty, his amazing ability to parse events to their most subtle moments, his miracles, his adeptness at guiding disciples through their own experience to the insight of understanding. Inspiring, yes; but is it available to us?

Then came Guru Padmasambhava (Guru Rinpoche), appearing a short time after the Buddha's Parinirvana, his life parallel in many ways to Shakyamuni Buddha's. There are places in Tibet, Nepal, and Bhutan that show handprints and footprints, some in unreachable places, left in rocks by Guru Rinpoche, signs of his transcendent power over reality as it appears to us. Is this just good story-telling? Maybe. However, if we look at histories of Tibetan masters since the time of Guru Rinpoche, we see many astonishing stories of their compassionate activity in which abilities that surpass the bounds of worldly competence are displayed. If lineages of Tibetan masters can perform awe-inspiring acts in order to benefit others, is it not possible for us also? How do we access these hidden powers?

All Buddhist practice guides one to some level of peace and harmony, first for one's self and then for others. In Vajrayana Buddhism, every aspect of one's life and activity is focused on the goal of the twofold purpose, benefitting self and others by awakening to the ultimate and absolute truth. In Vajrayana Buddhism, there are countless practices that lead one to this accomplishment. Within each practice, there are certain common underlying components without which accomplishment will not be achieved. One of these is Guru Yoga, the practice of mingling one's mind with the mind of the Guru, the supreme spiritual guide. The teacher-student relationship is so critical to the success of one's practice that teachers and students are advised to examine each other for three to nine years before committing to each other: the teacher to make sure the student is a suitable vessel; the student to be certain of the teacher's qualities and pure intention. The student commits to following the teacher's guidance to the very best of his or her ability. The teacher commits to finding that student in every future lifetime until s/he has accomplished the goal of supreme enlightenment. The teacher's mind is understood to be the door of liberation: the state of enlightenment manifests when the student's mind becomes non-dual with the teacher's.

Realization of this non-dual state is the aim of the traditional Guru Yoga practice consisting of devotional and supplication prayers, and mantra recitation in many various forms.

INTRODUCTION

Perhaps if we had a culture and a lifestyle that allowed us to sit on our cushions for hours, days, weeks, and years, these beautiful prayers alone would penetrate our hearts and cause the great compassion to fully blossom in our mindstreams. However, as Westerners, it is extremely rare for us to have that opportunity. How fortunate for us that when a teacher finds us in a time and place that doesn't uphold that kind of spiritual immersion, she can put the teachings and the practice in a context that is accessible to us and our lifestyle.

Whether we practice on our cushion every day or not, whether we have made a physical connection with a spiritual guide or not, whether we practice Vajrayana Buddhism or not, *Viewing the Guru Through the Lens of the Seven Limb Puja* shows us how to transcend the human habits that keep us from knowing and experiencing the ultimate state of being, our own true nature. If we acknowledge that everything we have tried to make us happy has so far been less than successful, and if we consider that the happiness of all is just as important as our own, the methods presented by Jetsunma Ahkön Norbu Lhamo in the following pages open new doors to us on our spiritual journey. If we practice them with courage and faith aspiring to end suffering in all its forms, we will experience profound change with the potential for ultimate awakening.

— Ani Rinchen Khandro

Viewing the Guru Through the Lens of the Seven Limb Puja

We will be thinking about how to deepen in our practice of Guru Yoga and how to practice with a deeper sense of view, with a more profound sense of view. The antidote that we're trying to apply is the one that addresses our superficiality. As materialists, as modern people, as sentient beings in general, we are very superficial. In fact, our superficiality is literally invisible to us simply because we have no sense of anything other than superficiality.

When you hear this teaching, you should listen with your doors open. That means don't just listen to it lightly the way most people do. Most people, when they listen to either a conversation or teaching, they listen to it just skimming the surface, picking out the main points. In this case you don't want to use that technique. While that's okay for ordinary listening, in this case you want to not only hear everything that is actually said, but at the same time you also want to try, in a deeper way, to understand the concept that's being presented. You want to receive the totality of the idea, not just the top of it. You don't want to try now to determine the most important parts. In other words, accept the entire teaching, and then later on, as you begin to digest it, you'll be able to determine the important parts more readily.

Generally, when we are in our normal waking consciousness, we think that we are with the Guru only when—and even this is questionable—only when we are praying or doing our practice. We visualize the Guru in front of us. We think the Guru must be here, by the force of our devotion. And that's appropriate. Then we think also that we are with the Guru whenever we see the Guru's face. We think that when the Guru is actually in the room and we see the face, we see the form, then we are with the Guru. Maybe if we see a picture of the Guru, we have a moment of devotion and perhaps we feel a connection because of our past practice. We think, "Oh, now we are with the Guru."

If we are to really examine the way that we are thinking at that point, it's extremely superficial. There's no view in that at all. It's completely inaccurate. If we think in that way, it shows us that we have not accomplished pure view. We have not accomplished a deeper view, a view that would give us an idea as to how to practice more deeply. We have to try to understand the meaning of our relationship with the Guru in the deepest possible sense. We try, hopefully, to move past our perception of the Guru as a person. This is our goal. This is what we're trying to do, generally speaking, in our devotional yoga. We are trying to see past the personality, past the superficiality, into a more profound understanding, a more profound view.

Let's go back to that question that we might have answered differently when we were thinking more superficially: When is it that we are with the Guru? We are with the Guru literally every moment that we have the Buddha nature. We are with the Guru so long as we appear in the world and have within us the Buddha seed. What it actually means is that the Guru represents for us all sources of refuge—all Lamas, all Buddhas, all Bodhisattvas—these three that arise from the primordial nature.

The Lama represents for us the Dharma, all of the Dharma, every word that has been uttered of Dharma teaching. The Lama represents for us as well the entire Sangha, every monk, every nun, every Lama that has ever taken robes, that has ever practiced the Dharma. The Lama represents all the meditational deities with all their qualities, activities, and all their particular incarnations. The Lama also represents all of the Dakinis and all of the Dharma protectors. When we think of the Lama, we think that everything that arises from the fundamental Buddha nature, from the pure primordial nature, which is our Buddha nature, is represented by the Lama. The Lama represents everything that arises from the mind of enlightenment.

The Lama does not represent those things that arise from samsara. The Lama does not represent those things that increase our five poisons, that increase our delusions. The Lama, therefore, cannot cause suffering. The Lama cannot cause an increase in ignorance. The Lama is not capable of giving rise to more suffering and more delusion. If somehow within the relationship that we have with our Lama there is some suffering, then we have to look to ourselves as having impure perception, incorrect view, incomplete understanding, and the tendency to project outward what is actually happening within our own minds.

The reason we know that the Lama cannot increase our suffering or our poisons, or harm us in any way, is that the Lama appears as a display arising from the very mind of enlightenment. Within the mind of enlightenment there is no cause for suffering. When we regard the Lama, we see that the causes for suffering, the seeds for suffering, are not there. However, when we regard our own mind and our own perception and the way that we think, yes indeed, the seeds for all suffering are within that. Because our normal waking consciousness, our ego, our samsaric nature, whatever it is that we think of as our ordinary self, does indeed arise from samsaric causes that we have created; and they are, for the most part, non-virtuous. We have not understood the view, nor have we understood any way to be happy. When it comes to our state and our mind, yes, there is the cause for suffering. When we look at the Guru we have to understand, that there, in that place, there is no cause for suffering.

This view is an antidote for practitioners who say they wish to completely open their hearts and minds to the Guru and practice surrender, but can't. They wish to really open their hearts to the Guru. They wish to receive the blessing without any obstacle, but are unable to because they have experienced trauma and hurt and different kinds of suffering associated with samsaric life. Think and concentrate on this: The Guru is that which arises from the mind of enlightenment and therefore does not have within it the causes for suffering. It is our own mind, our own perception, our own samsaric personality/ego structure—not our enlightened nature—that has within it all the causes for suffering.

Because we can perceive anything any way we want, we are likely to experience suffering. Even if it seems as though we experience suffering from an enlightened source, we know that this cannot be so. Learning to understand what that actually means for us is the first step in learning how to practice spiritual surrender.

We have to give up our old habit of blame. We have to attain self-honesty—now comes the time when we actually need it. We will depend on self-honesty to avoid the tendency to place blame on something external. If we have not attained any self-honesty, the pain that we suffer, the trauma that we live through still comes from "out there." Once we have learned self-honesty, we understand that our suffering comes from our own inability to practice those causes which create happiness. We accept personal responsibility for our own unhappiness.

What is it that we actually see when we see the Guru? First of all, the Guru is perfection, the Guru is perfect. The Guru arises very naturally, is spontaneously liberated. There is nothing about this appearance that has become tainted or impure. There is no conceptualization. There is no contrivance at all. We are seeing a natural display of the primordial wisdom state. We are literally seeing, in a non-dual way, the union of emptiness and luminosity.

Because of our samsaric minds, we are not able to understand the non-duality of emptiness and luminosity. We are simply not able to understand. To us they appear as two nouns. Emptiness is emptiness. We can describe that. Luminosity is luminosity. Maybe we can describe that. Emptiness and luminosity are non-dual. The best we can do is maybe to say it real quick. That's about as good as we can do!

What is this non-dual display, this non-duality called emptiness and luminosity? First of all, the Lama represents the primordial empty nature, which is completely free of any kind of distinction or contrivance, any kind of ideation, any color, any form, anything that becomes something. The Lama is the display of that which is without beginning and without end, of that which is primordially pure with no change, no movement, no contrivance, no distinguishing factors whatsoever. The Lama represents that pure emptiness. When we talk about emptiness in that way, Americans have a difficult time. That's why I'm trying to explain it in common ways, rather than using traditional buzz words.

When we think of emptiness, we think of a minus in a sense; like an empty room is a room without things in it. We think an empty glass is a glass without liquid in it. That's the way that we understand emptiness. Instead, you should understand that emptiness doesn't mean an absence of. Emptiness in this case is more like freedom, more like liberation: liberation from conceptualization, liberation from contrivance. The mind does not hold anything in a package. Here, emptiness is liberation. Supposing you were capable at this moment of losing all the fetters, allowing the mind to abide spontaneously, allowing the mind to simply rest in wakefulness? Rest in wakefulness. That is perhaps the closest we can come to understanding emptiness.

When we think about luminosity, we think about it as a plus, like a light being on. A light is on or it's off. Luminosity is something we think of as, well, luminous, so it may be glowing. Of course that's not what we're talking about here either. Let's say we could attain in our practice the true understanding of emptiness. If we could rest in innate wakefulness, free of contrivance, free of any kind of distinction or super-structuring or building or grasping or clinging... Try to imagine a mind such as that: innately wakeful. Then supposing that nature, free of contrivance, were to show itself in a gossamer, free light... I can't find the word that I'm looking for. Maybe the word only exists in my mind. Maybe there isn't such a word. Buoyant? Maybe buoyant. If you can combine all those words, you might have the right word. This is a problem for Buddhism in this country. We're going to have to create another language.

What if we were to imagine something from the profound innate wakefulness that is empty of contrivance, a display that showed itself as inseparable from that nature in every single sense, not separate whatsoever. That display was not leaving the state of emptiness in order to show itself, but was completely indistinguishable from emptiness, in the same way that the sun's rays are completely indistinguishable from the sun itself. There is no way to tell what is actually the tight, hard ball of the sun, and what is the light and heat that comes out of it. There is no way to tell the difference. If we could imagine such a display, we might call that luminosity.

We might say that this profound view of emptiness, this

innate wakefulness that is complete and yet unbegun, could somehow show its face in a gossamer, uncontrived, inseparable display that can't be called light, can't be called movement, can't be called anything because it has not moved out of that nature. But because we need to use a word, we say luminosity, and we must understand that this emptiness and luminosity are indistinguishable from one another. We must understand that this is what the Lama actually represents.

Therefore, the Lama represents the primordial wisdom state—that which is the wakefulness of Buddhahood in dance, in display, and in radiance—not separate from the innate nature, yet arising in a completely pure display that is indistinguishable from primordial nature. That is what the Lama actually is.

The Lama represents the union of emptiness and movement, or display. The Lama represents the union of wisdom and method. Guru Rinpoche always appears to us with the Dakini. He is always in union with the Dakini. Even when we see him in pictures or statues appearing to be alone, he has the symbol of the Dakini in the cleft of his left arm. In his nature he is never without the Dakini. That is a very profound teaching as to how to understand the Lama.

The Lama is understood as the appearance of the primordial nature, and the display of that nature appearing in our world, in our eyes, in our samsaric existence. The Lama represents the union of emptiness and luminosity.

When we meditate on Buddhahood, when we contemplate on what it would be like to achieve realization, when we think about these teachings that we have been given, when we try to simply abide spontaneously in our meditation, what do we think we are after? What do we think the result will be? Eventually, through the force of our practice, we are hoping that someday we will awaken as the Buddha has awakened. And if we practice well, this will surely be the result. We are actually looking to give rise to the very same thing that we are looking at when we see the Guru. We are looking to give rise to the primordial empty nature. We are looking to give rise to this nature which is free of contrivance, which is free of distinction, this primordial empty nature that is the innate nature, the Buddha nature. We are trying to give rise to that in such a way that it appears, even within samsara. We wish to attain realization now. It is this very union of emptiness and display, of emptiness and luminosity, of wisdom and method, that we wish to give rise to in our practice. This is the ultimate object of refuge.

From the Vajrayana point of view, we are told that we will never achieve realization without the necessary ripening that is provided by the Root Guru. We are told that in our practice we are dependent upon the Root Guru to transmit this blessing and to lead us through the door of liberation. We must understand that it is more than that. Practicing devotion in this way opens the door, creates the connection, creates the habit, creates the karma, creates the cause by which we will awaken to our own primordial wisdom nature. That nature will appear in samsara as the enlightened appearance. This is the goal; this is the very wish. The Lama, understood in that way, becomes the center of the mandala of our practice, of our hope, of our prayers, of our devotion, of our lives. The Lama becomes the very core of our lives. Understand there is never a time, never a moment, that you are not in the presence of the Lama.

If you refuse, if you're ignorant, if you doubt, if through habit you ignore, if through slothfulness you simply put no effort into accomplishing that view, then you are not actually turning away from the Guru as a person out there. This is not an act that is happening between you and somebody else. You are not slighting the person that is sitting on the throne. This is not what's happening. What's happening is that you are turning your own mind away from the very face of your enlightenment, away from your nature. You are splitting yourself away from salvation. You are rending yourself away from the very hope that will bring future happiness and realization. You are cutting yourself away from the root of your accomplishment.

Now that I have told you this, you cannot in good faith and good conscience remain superficial in your practice any longer. You must understand that every time you push away the Lama in order to live your ordinary samsaric mental posture, you are spitting in the face of your own Buddha seed. You are turning away from primordial emptiness, from the Buddha nature, from the pure luminosity that is the very display of that nature, that luminosity that we also know as the Bodhicitta.

You have abandoned the root of your accomplishment. You have abandoned the very milk of your nature, and you have shut the door to the great Bodhicitta. This is what we do when we forget and deny that we are always sitting at the feet of the Guru. We must always be looking into the eyes of the Guru. We have to train ourselves to keep the Guru above the crown of our heads, on the throne within our hearts, in our eyes, in our ears, in our hands. We have to train ourselves as though we are some kind of precious vessel that is carrying around this most precious nectar of enlightenment. We can't spill a drop, neither can we turn away from it. We've spilled so many drops already.

Now that we know what we have in our hands, as practitioners who now have moved from childhood to adulthood, we expect ourselves not to drop the ball, not to drop our practice. Whereas before, we were like children. When we teach children to prostrate, we do not worry whether their form is perfect. When we teach them to say mantra, we know they're going to make mistakes. But now we're moving past that regarding our devotional yoga. We can no longer allow ourselves to be the children that we once were.

WHAT DO WE OFFER THE GURU?

*'What we have offered the Guru are five cups;
five cups of poison.'*

Offering the Cup of Hatred

We have made many offerings to the Guru. Mostly, what we have offered the Guru are five cups: five cups of poison. We have offered the Guru hatred, because there in the presence of the primordial nature, there in the presence of the display of the Bodhicitta, there in that non-dual pristine purity, we have—without shame—hated, abused, neglected. We have committed horrible sins against others who are innocent, against motherly sentient beings. Not only in this lifetime, but previously as well. We have done this bold-faced in the presence of that which is so holy as to be indescribable.

Offering the Cup of Greed and Grasping

We have offered the cup of greed and grasping. Every single day in the presence of our own mind, in the face of the Guru, in the great silent sound of primordial emptiness, in the great quiet light of the display of luminosity, right there in the place of Bodhicitta, from our mouth where the speech of comfort should come, instead we have offered the cup of greed. This is what we have offered the Guru. This is the offering that we have made.

Without shame, we grasp; we are filled with greed. We do nothing but think about me, me, me, and what can I have, and what can I do, and how great am I. Don't you want to give me some more approval? Don't you want to give me some more? This is what we do in the face of the Guru.

Offering the Cup of Ignorance

The third cup that we offer to the face of the Guru is ignorance, our ignorance. We begin our lives with ignorance, which is forgivable. At five or six years old we come to consciousness. Later on we figure out that we're as dumb as posts. We are ignorant; we just don't have the teaching yet.

Now we have come to the point where we have received the teaching. We have received enough of the teaching that, while we still abide in samsara, we are moving away from ignorance. We are bringing down or quelling the poison of ignorance. Yet in the face of the Guru, in the face of the primordial empty nature that is our nature, in the face of the very display of Bodhicitta, we have willfully remained ignorant. Willfully. We have not accomplished our practice; we have turned away from our practice. We have not tried very hard. We have not listened to the teachings. We continue to listen to the teachings as though they were water rolling off our back. We have not taken the advice of our Gurus.

What Do We Offer the Guru?

Imagine that you had one chance to listen to Guru Rinpoche. That was the only contact with Dharma that you were ever going to have in your whole life, and Guru Rinpoche offered to give you the keys to liberation, to everything that you need. What would that listening look like? Hopefully, if you are not stupider than a post, you would listen to the Guru's teachings as though they were your very breath. You would listen with your whole heart and every word would be like food, like nectar to you. You would take every bit of it home and work with it all the time. If that were the only opportunity you would ever have to receive these teachings from Guru Rinpoche, maybe you might think like that. But in the face of our Root Guru that's not what we do. I used to ask my students what the teaching was about, but I stopped that because it used to break my heart when there was no answer.

We are faulted in the way that we make offerings. We cling to our ignorance. We have heard the method and have heard the teachings. Yet we do not practice accordingly, to the best of our abilities. We have offered the cup of ignorance to our Guru; and that is the best we could do.

Offering the Cup of Jealousy

The next cup that we have offered to the Guru is jealousy. Boldly, in the face of our very nature, in the very display of Bodhicitta, we have looked at the accomplishments of others and have said, "I can do that." We have competed and we have been jealous. We have looked to others' belongings and we have said, "I wish I had that instead of you." We try to make ourselves feel better: we practice self-aggrandizement, we lift ourselves up, and put others down. These things we have done in the very face of the Guru who is indistinguishable from us, from our nature, and from the nature of all beings.

There is only the nature. It's not divided into pigeon holes. It's not like an ice-cube tray that's divided into sections. When we look into the face of any motherly sentient being and perform our usual ritual of jealousy and competitiveness, we are actually playing this game with the Root Guru. Therefore, we have in truth been jealous and competitive toward the Root Guru, because there is no distinction. If we think that it's okay to be that way in front of other sentient beings but not okay to be that way in front of the Guru, then we are holding up the cup of ignorance as well. We should know better than that. We have been taught more than that. By now we know that all sentient beings have within them the Buddha nature, the Buddha seed, and that is inseparable from the Guru's nature. If we harm, ignore, treat badly or abuse others, this is what we have done to the Guru. We have held up the cup of jealousy.

Offering the Cup of Pride

The last wonderful offering that we have made to the Guru is the cup of pride. In front of the Guru, that all-pervasive nature which is fundamentally undifferentiated, innately pure, and spontaneously liberated, which is free of any kind of conjecture, contrivance, or distinction, in front of that pure display we have held ourselves up as great, as special, as superior. We have held ourselves up as that which requires special attention, as that which requires approval because we are so wonderful. We have not been ashamed, in front of the face of the Guru, to indicate that we are superior to others. We have not been ashamed to do that.

Strangely, we feel shame and embarrassment at the idea of surrender in devotion, but to show our pride, our stinking nasty pride, in front of the face of the Guru, *that* we have no shame about. That doesn't bother us at all. Our thinking is completely backwards, completely backwards.

This is not good news. We like to come to class and hear good inspiring things so we can come away with that shot in the arm. And for the next week or so we can behave ourselves—maybe. That's what we like to do. We like to be entertained. This is not the kind of thing that we like to hear. But if you really are honest with yourself, you know that what I am saying is true. What if Guru Rinpoche himself, appearing in a way that you could understand, were to actually walk through every day with you? What if he could see what is in your mind, in your heart, walk through all your efforts, watch you when you turn away and say, "Okay, that's enough of that. I'm going to do what I want to do. Enough of that high thinking; let me feel the way that I naturally feel. The hell with you."

If you could actually feel the eyes of the Guru watching you, if you had felt that even for one day, there would never be an end to your grief. There would never be an end to the sorrow that you would feel knowing, that in the face of the Guru, you had made such a stinking offering. We remain content with our self-cherishing, content with our pride, content with our ego, our hatred, our bigotry, and our bad qualities. We remain content with these while the Guru watches. There is no moment that you are alive in samsara that the eyes of the Guru are not watching. I don't mean like a little kid thinking that mommy's watching. It's not like that.

The Guru doesn't get mad at you. It isn't an approval thing. It isn't like your mother; it's not like your father. It's that the eyes of the Guru are like a radiant connection through which we can directly see the primordial nature, which is free of any kind of contrivance, separation, ugliness, or superficiality. It is free of any of the possibilities that make it likely that we are going to practice any kind of non-virtue. This nature is so pure that it's like having the eyes of supreme un-nameable, unspeakable sweetness looking at us always, looking at us with love and compassion. We are taking shit and throwing it against the wall and wiping it all over ourselves, scratching and burping and farting, and hitting and killing and carrying on. Yet these eyes hold us up. They watch us always, even while we, like apes in a zoo, fling shit on them.

Yet we wonder why it is that we cannot awaken to the Buddha nature. When is IT going to happen? When is IT going to happen to me? When is IT going to come from out there? How old am I going to be when IT happens? As though it were going to be visited upon you like something air-dropped. As though it were going to come to you from another city, another state, or another world. All the time we are turning away from those eyes, those loving, perfect, pure eyes that are actually like guiding beams of light.

Turning Away from the Guru

*'The moment we turn away from the face of the Guru
and find something else, in that moment we have
turned away from the primordial nature that
is our nature, and found suffering.'*

When we turn our face away from the Guru, we are only creating more suffering. There is no other result that can come from that, no matter what it looks like. You might say there are extenuating circumstances. All right, name them! I'd like to see an extenuating circumstance that's going to change what I've just said, because it doesn't exist. You might say, "Oh well, you know, yes, I did my practice from this time to this time, and I really tried very hard with my Guru Yoga. I worked very hard at that, and I kept it mindful as much as I could, and then… Well, you know, I have other things to do. I have to go work, and I have to go do this, and I have to go do that." This is the kind of thinking that we have.

While we are in the state of devotional practice, aware of being in the presence of the Guru, practicing that kind of view, we create only causes of future bliss and happiness. The moment we turn away saying, "Okay, that's that. Now on to this," we practice the non-virtue which causes us unthinkable suffering in this and every life that we have experienced. The moment we turn away from the face of the Guru and find something else, in that moment we have turned away from the primordial nature that is our nature, and found suffering.

The moment that we go on to the next thing is the moment that we go on to our suffering. The moment that we move away from our practice into another state is when we move away from what causes bliss and move into what will only bring about more suffering, even if our activity is just as pure and clean as apple pie. Let's say we ended our practice to go feed the baby. You can't argue with that. You have to feed babies, right? Of course you've got to feed the baby. The problem is turning away from the Guru in order to do it.

You haven't actually figured all of this out yet. It's time to practice so deeply that you understand that it is possible not to turn away, ever. It is possible to be in that space, to be with that face, to be of that face, to be inseparable, to be constantly in union with that which is union itself—to be inseparable with the Guru. This is the goal. Why wouldn't it be the goal? Is it from samsara that you wish to be inseparable? Is it suffering? Is it non-virtue? Do you like to turn away? Maybe you like the result, the suffering that comes after.

Now that I say it this way, it seems ridiculous! Of course you don't want that! Yet in our practice, in our lives, what do we do? We offer the five cups of poison. This is our standard offering every day. Then we read the text and it says that if we could just offer one butter lamp, we would remain in immovable samadhi. We wonder, "I've offered lots of butter lamps! What is the hold-up? What's the problem?" I'll tell you what the problem is. It's those five other cups that you offer so much more of than that butter lamp.

Maybe the butter lamp needs to be understood as a symbol. Maybe the butter lamp needs to be understood not only as a literal butter lamp on an altar, but maybe like a light in the window, a constant reminder. If you know that a loved one is nearby and you're trying to guide them home, you'd keep a light on, wouldn't you? Maybe that's what we need to do. Maybe it's like that. Maybe the butter lamp we need to offer, the one that brings us to immovable samadhi, is the light that never extinguishes, the light of recognition.

It's so silly, isn't it? Here we are talking about the Lama as being our own precious nature. Someday when we die and all the elements fall away, what will arise naturally is the natural state of uncontrivance. For practitioners there is realization, simply because for the practitioner, if we have meditated properly, we will recognize that natural uncontrived state as the very primordial mother from which we have sprung. Like a child who has been separated from his mother for a while, who runs to the mother with such happiness and joy, it practically rips open his heart. The child sits on the mother's lap and doesn't wish to separate from the mother at all. Like that, if we are meditators, we will go to that nature. We will recognize with fervent regard, but so much more than that—I don't even have the words.

Here in our lives, due to the force of merit that we have accumulated in the past—that same pristine quality of uncontrived nature appears in samsara to speak to us, to see us with its eyes, to hold our hand, to teach us how to practice with recognition—yet, we're drunk, light in the head, stupid. We're like that. We can't care, we can't get it together. Our minds are just weak that way.

Even with all of our terrible practice, we are still hoping that when we die and those elements begin to disintegrate and fall away, that somehow, we will recognize the primordial wisdom nature. Boy, are we thinking like Peter Pan. That's what I call magical thinking. The only way it is going to happen is to begin to recognize that nature now. The only proper way to recognize the nature of the Guru is to simultaneously recognize our own nature, and to know that they are indistinguishable. If we look at the Guru and find fault, that means we are acting with samsaric intention, with samsaric mind, and the result is samsara. There is no practice there. We do that every moment. That's not practice. But if we think and practice in the way that I've just discussed, then instead when we see the Guru we see the face of salvation. We see literally, "I am that. That I am." Even there, of course, you can't say "I;" "I" separates us. But in the beginning we have the intention of understanding: That which is the nature is my nature also. Instead of judgment and hatred, instead of greed and ignorance, instead of jealousy and pride, inside there is a soundless chant that says, "Holy, holy, holy." And that is practice.

Applying the Seven Limb Puja

In that case, what are the postures that we should take, constantly, every moment, every day? Since we find that we are in the presence of the primordial Guru at every single moment, what is the posture that we should take? The *Seven Limb Puja*[1] appears in many different practices in slightly different variations, but it has certain common denominators. These should be studied and looked at as a guide to practice now that one is coming to understand that the eyes of the Guru are our eyes; that the heart of the Guru is our heart; that our nature is the nature. We are indistinguishable from that.

Paying Homage

> *'Paying homage is the antidote that gives rise to that spiritual posture that makes it possible to recognize the nature of the Guru...'*

Practicing in that way, we should think like this: First of all, knowing that the face of the Guru is always with us, we

---

[1] The Tibetan text, transliteration and English translation of the Seven Limb Puja from the Gandavyuha chapter of the Avatamsaka Sutra, can be found on pages 55-62. Excerpts from that original text are highlighted throughout Jetsunma's teaching that follows.

Paying Homage

Throughout all the worlds in the ten directions,
Dwell the sugatas of the three times, lions among men,
To all of them without exception
With devotion I bow down with my body, speech and mind.
By the strength of this aspiration to the deeds of the excellent,
And by envisioning myself in the presence of all the victorious ones,
Prostrating to them with bodies as numberless as the atoms of this world,
I pay homage to every Buddha!
Upon each atom are as many Buddhas as atoms exist,
Each seated in the midst of gathered Bodhisattvas.
In this way the entire Dharmadhatu excluding nothing
Is imagined to be completely filled by victorious ones.
Rendering praises inexhaustible as the ocean.
In melodious tones as boundless as the sea,
The enlightened qualities of all the conquerors are acknowledged.
And I praise all Sugatas!

should practice constantly paying homage to the Guru. This antidotes our pride, our ego, that habit that says, "Oh, well look at that! The Guru has faults. The Guru must be human." That is the statement that keeps us from practicing pure devotion and pure surrender, and prevents us from achieving realization. Paying homage is the antidote that gives rise to that spiritual posture that makes it possible to recognize the nature of the Guru as the absolute non-dual display of emptiness and luminosity and to give rise to profound devotion at last, rather than the superficial stuff that we've been passing off as devotion.

We practice paying homage. We pay homage to the Buddhas and the Bodhisattvas. The Lamas, of course, are in that number. The Buddhas and Bodhisattvas are all represented in the Lama. We pay homage to the Buddhas because they have crossed the ocean of suffering. Therefore, they are capable of captaining us across the ocean of suffering. We pay homage with that kind of regard: As though we need to cross an ocean of suffering, and the trip is scary and long, hazardous and difficult. We can't make it without a qualified captain. That is the kind of recognition of the superior quality of the Buddhas and Bodhisattvas, of the Lama, that we need. Recognize every moment. This is a vajra command: Recognize every moment. When we think of ourselves in our samsaric state and then we think of the Guru, we should think that the Guru is like a precious diamond, beyond compare, because the Guru is capable of helping us cross the ocean of suffering. We cannot do that by ourselves. That will antidote the kind of pride that we have when we try to put ourselves above everything, in subtle or gross ways.

Making Offerings

Excellent garlands of magnificent flowers,
Instrumentation, oils and the best of parasols,
Splendid butter lamps and sacred incense,
All of this is offered to the victorious ones (Buddhas)!
The finest of garments and superior perfumes
And fragrant powder equalling Sumeru,
This magnificent array of the finest and best of them all
Is offered to the victorious ones (Buddhas)!
Whatever is offered is unsurpassed in opulence
And directed with utmost devotion to all the Buddhas.
By the strength of faith of this aspiration of the deeds of excellence,
Paying homage to all the Buddhas, these offerings are made.

Making Offerings

'When we offer to the objects of refuge we are doing so for our sake, not for their sake.'

Secondly, in the face of the Guru we should always be making offerings. Do you make offerings when you come to temple? Nice, but not enough. Do you make offerings when you put water into the little bowls on your altars in the morning? Nice, but not enough. Do you make offerings of the first portions of your food? Great, but not enough. We should be making offerings constantly. But how can we do that? You think, "Oh, my hands are busy. I can't always be making offerings." Therefore, most of the offerings are going to be mental offerings. If we are making mental offerings appropriate to the information that I have just given you—that the Guru's face is indistinguishable from our own nature, and we are always in the presence of the Guru in the same way that we are always in the presence of the nature—then there should never be a moment that we do not make offerings.

What would that look like? How could you practice that way? In the face of the Guru you must not grasp or cling to anything. Anything. That means if you smell something and it's a delicious smell, you offer it immediately, rather than keeping it for yourself. You know how when we smell food we go, "Umm, delicious! I'm keeping that, that's mine!" Instead of doing that, you smell it, you enjoy it, and you offer that nectar to the Lama. Every smell that is beautiful—even smells that are not beautiful—you think of as being instantly transformed into the very essence of bliss, and offer that to the Guru.

Offer everything that you see. We walk outside like we own the day. Our eyes drink it in. That's how we enjoy the day. We eat it up. The habit of greed is so strong. Remember that you are in the presence of the Guru constantly, that the Guru literally abides within your channels, winds, and fluids, within your psychic, spiritual, inner structure. That nature, which is your nature, is the Guru. Whenever you see something with your eyes that is beautiful, instantly offer your eyes, offer the vision, offer the feeling, and offer the pleasure of that to the Lama, to the holy one who has crossed the ocean of suffering for your sake. Instantly offer it up.

In the beginning, while getting into the habit, we are a little spastic and a little nuts. But later it becomes a natural, graceful, spontaneous movement. We actually change the way our perception works. It takes a little time, it takes some practice; but there will come a day when naturally you do not cling to your sight. Yes, you still see things. Yes, they register in your brain. Yes, your pupils and your irises work just right. The difference is that there is a graceful movement of offering that naturally occurs, as though you didn't grab onto everything in front of you. Do you remember when you first started practicing Bodhicitta, and you didn't feel like it? Like, "Yeah, I'm grateful to all motherly sentient beings. May they all rest in peace," in the same tone of voice that you would say, "Rot in Hell!" That's kind of what we did when we first started practicing Bodhicitta and we didn't have the habit of it. After a time it becomes more natural, doesn't it? It becomes more natural to think kindly, to think of compassion regarding other sentient beings.

It's like that with your perception. Make offerings constantly to the Buddhas and Bodhisattvas, to the Lama who embodies all the objects of refuge. Anything that you receive, consistently offer. It doesn't mean that you don't get to keep it. We are not looking at this in a limited, superficial way. We know that the Buddhas and Bodhisattvas actually don't need our offerings. They are content and complete. They are perfect. When we offer to the objects of refuge we are doing so for our sake, not for their sake. Isn't that true? Obviously then, if you make an offering, it probably won't disappear.

Ultimately, we think that whatever we have belongs to the Buddhas and the Bodhisattvas. We have given everything that we own. There is a posture of peacefulness and lack of tension regarding personal possessions that naturally occurs over time. We begin to think that it's already been offered, and therefore there's nothing to cling to. Slowly, slowly, over time, we develop that habit. The habit becomes very real, and our minds become very smooth and more joyful. Actually, it isn't having that makes us joyful; it is freedom from the need to have that makes us happy.

We make constant offerings because we are constantly in the presence of the Guru. We should think that in the presence of the primordial empty nature, non-dual as the display of luminosity—here in the presence of the fundamental Bodhicitta, the miraculous Bodhicitta, the unbelievably potent, pure, uncontrived Bodhicitta—it is simply not appropriate to cling and grasp. It simply isn't appropriate. It becomes filthy and disgusting. Supposing Guru Rinpoche were sitting right in front of you, and you were given some tea or food. Would you be like,

Confession

Overpowered by desire, anger and delusion,
With my body, my speech and similarly with my mind,
Whatever negativity that I have amassed,
I confess individually and entirely.

"Gimme, gimme"? How could you even think of eating with Guru Rinpoche in front of you? You would offer, "Please take. Please take everything that I have! Please eat. Please let me offer this to you!" You'd think like that.

We must think, that in fact, this is the case—always with us is the precious Bodhicitta, always with us is the Lama. It is never appropriate to grasp. It is never appropriate to keep for ourselves what should naturally be offered. We get ourselves into the habit and the grace of constant offering.

Confession

> *'There is a natural to-the-bone honesty of realizing that you are a being wandering lost in samsara...'*

We should always be in the posture of confession. Confession need not be heard by any other person. When I first taught about confession, there was a line of people waiting to confess to me. I thought I was going to have to build one of those booths! In fact, confessions need not be done in front of anyone else. We're talking about spiritual confession now. One should always be in the posture of confession. Why is that so?

We know that since beginningless time until we received the teachings, we tried to be happy, but did not know how. Isn't that right? That means there's a pretty good chance we blew it big time. Judging from the fact that we are still suffering in samsara, we know that's true. We know that at least 50% of the time, we have committed non-virtuous acts—at least 50% of the time—just by the law of chance. Supposing you came to see the Guru, but you had walked through mud and had mud and junk all over you. Maybe you even had…oh, this is really disgusting, shit in your pants. Well, that's what we did until we got the teachings. We just shit in our pants. We didn't care. We didn't know. So you've got a load, one of those things that kids have when they look like…well, you know what they look like. Have you ever seen a kid with a low-slung diaper? We're walking in like that! We stink, and we're nasty. If you were going to see Guru Rinpoche, don't you think you would clean up a bit?

Think of confession in the exact same way. Think that you're always in the face of the Guru, always in the presence of that primordial nature. Yet you know that to simply fake it and put on a pseudo-spiritual face is not going to cut it. You're not looking at an ordinary being. You're not looking at something samsaric that wouldn't know the difference. You are in the presence of the primordial wisdom nature. All things are revealed. It doesn't mean that you're constantly repeating verbal confessions in your head. That would make you nuts, especially if you're trying to offer and pay homage at the same time.

The posture of confession is a little bit different. Here we're talking about subtleties. For the first time in our samsaric lives, we are not trying to hide our non-virtue and play the game of acting spiritual. There is a natural to-the-bone honesty of realizing that you are a being wandering lost in samsara, realizing what it took to get that lost in samsara, and realizing that's why you're in samsara. With that kind of awareness, there is the profound wish for all such causes of suffering, all such non-virtue, to be purified. That would be like a posture of confession: I know that I have engaged in non-virtuous conduct of all kinds. I have no illusions, and I do not try to pretend or shut it down or make nicey-nicey with my superficial face. I do not pretend that none of this has happened. I am truly, within the deepest part of my heart, a penitent person. I am constantly in that posture. I realize that I have performed non-virtue. In the face of the Guru, I wish to hold that up, like holding dewdrops up to the sun. That sun, the face of the Guru, has the same capacity as the sun in the sky. By the light of midday, those dewdrops will all be gone—if we don't hide them under a rock, pretend they don't exist, or put them away somewhere—but hold them up in the act of penitence, compassion, and honesty. We hold them up with complete confidence that this non-dual emptiness and luminosity, like the sun, will burn away all such poison.

Our posture—rather than committing that horrible non-virtue of doing shuck and jive, of trying to pretend that we're goody two-shoes—is a posture of honesty. In that posture of honesty, the heart is relaxed and the mind is opened. The non-virtue begins to evaporate like the dewdrops.

Rejoicing

'We are constantly rejoicing so that there is no room for grasping, clinging, judging, and all those things that we normally do.'

The next posture that we need to maintain constantly is that of rejoicing. Constantly rejoice. This posture of rejoicing actually isn't walking around being happy. It's not like that. That's putting a false face on, like we were just talking about. You have all this samsaric past in you and yet you're putting this happy face on it; kind of like the yellow smiley-faced guy

Rejoicing

The merit of all the victorious ones of the ten directions and their heirs,
Of the solitary realizers and those on the paths of learning
and no more learning,
And of every sentient being without exception—
I fully rejoice in all such accumulations!

with the eyes and the big smile.

That's not what we're talking about. We're talking about rejoicing in the accomplishments of the Buddhas and the Bodhisattvas, of all those who have achieved realization. We're talking about rejoicing in the accomplishments of others. In the face of the Guru, as that which is inseparable from the Guru's nature, we say, "Oh, this one has crossed the ocean of suffering," and we rejoice in that accomplishment. The accomplishment of the Guru reflects on our karma, if you think about it: I rejoice in the accomplishment of the Guru, and I am in the presence of the Guru, and the accomplishment of the Guru then becomes available to me as well.

How do you think the accomplishment of the Guru could ever become available to you if you do not rejoice in that respectfully? If you do not give rise to the recognition of that, the joy of that? If you say, "I wonder what she has really accomplished. Let's think about it. She really doesn't pay much attention to facts. She doesn't know any of those lists." You know, those Buddhist lists that everyone should know. You might be saying to yourself, "She doesn't know any of those lists. How good can she be?" Right, she doesn't have any laundry lists. That's the kind of thought that you might have about your teacher. Maybe in this case, you would be right. But in this case, it would be wrong for you, because it doesn't help you to think like that! If you find fault in the face of your Guru, you'll never achieve realization. Period. That's it.

If you don't recognize the nature of the Guru, you cannot recognize your own nature. It simply will not occur. Instead, we recognize the qualities of the Guru. We see that the Guru is the very extension of Guru Rinpoche's miraculous compassion, that the Guru is primordial empty nature and luminosity, nondual, expressed in the world in a form that we can understand. This form is beyond flaw. It is not a human being. It is not a samsaric being. It is not a prop. It is not a thing. It is not out there. It is the very display of our nature in a form that we can recognize. We rejoice in that.

That's how rejoicing is relevant to our practice. In general, rejoicing in the welfare of those who have accomplished Dharma includes rejoicing in the Buddhas who have crossed the ocean of suffering and returned for the sake of sentient beings, rejoicing in the Bodhisattvas who hold back from the brink of nirvana for the sake of sentient beings, rejoicing even in practitioners who are now accomplishing Dharma in order to benefit sentient beings. When one of your peers has completed Ngöndro or some other practice, or had a really profound relation with their practice and are really moving on, the human tendency would be to say, "Well, I could do that." Or maybe, if not that, our tendency is to say, "Well, yeah, they're practicing all day, but you never see them take out the garbage or wash the dishes." That's the kind of tendency that we have. Instead, we are talking about constantly rejoicing in the achievements of others. That is a way to increase your own accomplishment as well.

In terms of practicing with the Guru, we should think that in fact we are looking at the face of primordial nature. We are looking at the nature of emptiness, at the display of luminosity that appears in the world. We are rejoicing in the accomplishment of the Guru, in the magical, mystical and miraculous appearance in the world for the sake of sentient beings. We are constantly rejoicing so that there is no room for grasping, clinging, judging, and all those things that we normally do.

Requesting Teachings

> *'The thing you have been terrified of, that you have guarded yourself against, is the very thing you should be requesting constantly.'*

We should also be in the posture of requesting teachings. Think about that. Many students will have what they think is a nice relationship with the Guru. They think, "I have a really good relationship with my teacher. I practice every day and I come to teachings and give offerings. My teacher smiles at me, and altogether, I would say that things are going pretty well." But that same student does not come to the teacher and throw open their heart and life and say, "Take me. Take me and change me and fill my life with your blessing." Actually, that's not entirely true. I've had quite a number of students come to me and say, "Oh Lama, make of me whatever I should be!" Their hair is nicely done and then they pose a little. You know, they do it from their best side! Watch me while I do this, Mommy! They do that with their mouth. But with their mind, with their hearts? Not once. Not ever. Not in any case have I had a student truly say to the Guru, "I request the nectar that you hold. I request what you have."

The reason is that we are still clinging to our ordinary samsaric experience, our ordinary samsaric lives. We say that we come to Dharma so that we can achieve realization. We

REQUESTING TEACHINGS

All those who illuminate the world systems of the ten directions,
Who have attained buddhahood and freedom from attachment
throughout the stages of enlightenment,
I implore all those protectors
To turn the peerless wheel of the Dharma!

come to Dharma so that we can change into a fully awakened realized being, but we don't want to change. How's that going to happen? It is illogical! It's never going to happen!

We find ourselves sitting at the feet of that miraculous appearance which somehow magically has appeared, even through the thickness of our non-virtue, the thickness of our karma, like the sun penetrating black storm clouds. Somehow the teacher has appeared. We know from the teachings that this is the very face of primordial wisdom nature. This is the very display of natural luminosity. This is the magical mystical appearance. Yet we go away from it. We say, "Okay, you want to give me this fabulous teaching? I'm going to really listen up to this, because I am a good girl." Then at the end of the teaching we close our minds, fold them up, and go home.

If we thought of the Guru as an ordinary being, then perhaps the only avenue open to us would be listening to teachings. We have just learned that we are looking into the face of our primordial nature. What are the limitations of that primordial wisdom nature? There are none whatsoever. Supposing then, we were in the posture of understanding in a deep and profound way the correct view of how to see, how to know, how to experience devotional yoga. We understand through correct view more deeply than we've ever understood before. That opens us up. Because in that case, we know that we are always in the presence of the primordial wisdom nature. We know that the display of Bodhicitta is always inseparable from us; that those eyes are on us, within us; that face lives within our psychic winds, channels, and fluids. You would always be in the posture of beseeching the Guru to never stop pouring forth the nectar of Dharma.

Constantly beseech the Guru to never stop, not for a moment. Whatever it takes, whatever it feels like, whatever it makes me think, or makes me look like, whatever happens, Lord Guru, please do not stop pouring the Dharma into my heart and my mind for one moment. You should think like that, because the moment that there is no Dharma being brought to you, then at that moment there is no cause for liberation occurring. If you are not giving rise to a constant love and regard for the nectar of the teacher, which is the Dharma, how are the causes for enlightenment going to occur? As Buddhists, we say that our only goal is to quit our wandering hopelessly in samsara, and to enter through the door of liberation. We wish to enter into the state which is beyond suffering for the sake of sentient beings. This should be our only true wish. Yet, we have our cut-off point. We say, "Enough. Thank you. That was a nice teaching. I'm going home now. See you."

Sometimes we receive the nectar, and sometimes the door is closed. Yet, if we understood that blessing in a deep way, that the Guru's nature is inseparable from our nature, we would realize that upon walking away from the teaching, or separating ourselves from the holy space where we are constantly drinking the nectar of enlightenment, at that very moment we have walked away and said, "See you" to our own primordial wisdom nature.

We throw up our hands and say, "How long, Buddha? How long will I have to go on without liberation?" At the same time, we walk away and do not wish to hear any more teaching. We want to revert back to our own minds and what we think and what we feel. We don't want any more nectar. Maybe we hear a class for two hours, and then we go away. How long is it until the next time we have contact with the teacher? In that time, have we been requesting teachings? Have we been drinking the nectar of the Guru constantly? No. No, because our view stinks. We haven't been in the presence of the body of the teacher, so we don't hear the words of the teacher.

If for two hours you had correct view listening to teachings, and for two hours you did some practice, then for four hours altogether you had some decent view, some regard, some devotion. Then the whole rest of the time in that twenty-four hour period, there's been no other practice. There's been nothing. There has been no requesting the nectar of the Guru, the nectar of Bodhicitta, the nectar of Dharma, to constantly pour into you. In essence then, your mind is closed. It's not open for business regarding Dharma. You wonder then why you spent two hours in class and two hours practicing. Are you closer to that precious moment of awakening? By four hours? Yes, four hours ahead, twenty hours behind. If you think of it in linear terms, then you've put your realization four hours closer, and twenty hours later. Is that the way you want to practice?

Of course, that's a linear view. It's a silly view, really, if we're talking from a more profound state of consciousness. But that's how we should think about it. It will be helpful in understanding that the kind of practice that results in supreme enlightenment is a continuous, natural, graceful effort. A happy, blissful, joyful continuous effort. Of course we can't be, "Oh, please Lama, give me teachings. Oh, please Lama, give me teachings. Oh, please Lama..."

It's not like that. You have to let go of that one. What I'm saying is that you are always in the posture of requesting teachings. That means you walk around with your heart, your mind like a bowl. You are in a posture of a constant wish, "Please Lord Guru, change me into whatever form is necessary. Change my mind. Change my heart. Purify my karma. Please Lord Guru, the only thing I ask you is to not let me remain the same. Please Lord Guru, constantly pour the nectar of your Dharma into me."

Think of the Guru like a mother bird. Think of yourself like a baby bird, always hungry, relying totally on the Guru not only to gather the food for you, but even to chew it up and push it into your mouth, because you are so weak you can hardly swallow. The way to remedy that weakness and that slothfulness in our practice is to constantly remain in the posture of beseeching the Guru for teachings. "Lord Guru, do not abandon me in samsara. Do not leave me in the condition that I am in now. Change me utterly and completely to where I do not recognize myself as an ordinary samsaric being any longer." The thing you have been terrified of, that you have guarded yourself against, is the very thing you should be requesting constantly—to be transformed and changed according to the wishes of the Guru. "Do not let me be separate from your teachings, not even for a moment."

One has to accomplish whatever teachings are given verbally by the teacher. One has to contemplate them, take them to heart, let them lie deeply within, rather than simply rolling off the skin. Inwardly, one's posture is constantly like a bowl. "Please, give me everything that you have. Not some, not a little, not as much as I can take. All of it!" Do you have the courage to do that? That's the kind of courage it takes to accomplish your practice.

Beseeching the Buddhas, Bodhisattvas, and Lamas to Remain

> *'We should be in the posture of constantly requesting the Buddhas and Bodhisattvas, those who have attained realization, to remain in the world.'*

The next posture we should keep ourselves in is beseeching the Buddhas, Bodhisattvas, and the Lamas to remain. Where would you be now if suddenly your Root Guru disappeared? You should ask that question of someone who has experienced the horrible, horrible occurrence of the death of their Guru. If you think practice is hard now, you should think what it must be like to go through the pain of knowing that your Guru is no longer in the world. Try to imagine how it would be if we have to reach into our practice even more deeply, in a more profound way, knowing that the Guru is no longer in the world. Knowing that there will not be physical teachings forthcoming, how can we find the Guru? It's very scary to think that there might be a time like that. How awful to not be in the physical presence, the here and now presence, with constant teachings occurring from the Guru in a physical way.

We should think like this: What would it be like if our Gurus had simply attained realization, and then gone on and remained in nirvana? Attained realization and then never appeared in samsara again? What would that be like? That would

BESEECHING THE BUDDHAS

All you who intend to display entering nirvana,
For the purpose of bringing benefit and bliss to all beings,
For as many eons as there are particles of dust on earth,
With palms pressed together I beseech you to remain in the world!

mean that in samsara there would be no teaching. There would be no method. There would be no means by which to accomplish Dharma. There would only be the means to accomplish non-virtue. There would be endless suffering compounded every single moment like a geometric progression—constantly increasing, with no leveling off, with no cessation, with no chance, no opportunity, and no change. Life would be constantly miserable. Only the results of the poisons—hatred, greed, ignorance, jealousy, pride, war, suffering—would be ripened. There would be no relief, no method by which to accomplish relief, no means by which to accomplish virtue. It is so unthinkable that we can't even imagine that.

Yet in our confusion, we can't even give a moment to think how miraculous it is that our Guru has returned to face us in the world—because we can't see the Guru in our mind, because we can't see the Guru in our inner channels, winds, and fluids, because we can't see the Guru in our nature. The Guru appears to us as the miraculous through the shit and thickness of our stinking delusions. We don't even have a minute to request that it will always be the case that the Gurus, the Buddhas, the Bodhisattvas will return for the sake of sentient beings. We never think how miraculous it is, how marvelous it is, how unequalled by any other gift or any other miracle. We are so concerned with our own superficial lives, we have not even a moment to spare to thank the teacher for returning to us. Think what they did! They did not pass into nirvana! It doesn't mean that they haven't accomplished their practice. It doesn't mean that they don't actually spontaneously abide in nirvana now. In fact, it means that they appear in the world under samsaric conditions for our sake. And we only have a minute a day to rejoice in that and request them to remain.

We should contemplate on what it would be like to remain in the world without any source of liberation. We should constantly be thinking what it would be like if the Buddhas and Bodhisattvas did not enter into the world for our sake, did not appear among us, as us, in a form that we could understand and empathize with. We should think what that would be like, and having contemplated on that, realize it would be unthinkable, horrible, and worse than any suffering we have ever experienced or could ever imagine experiencing. Try to imagine what it would be like with no help.

With the force that comes from that contemplation, every time we see our teacher, we should think, "Please remain in the world. Oh, please remain in the world. Oh, please remain in the world." We should be thinking like that when we say our teachers' long life prayers. We should be in the posture of constantly requesting the Buddhas and Bodhisattvas, those who have attained realization, to remain within the world.

How would we be constantly requesting that? By expressing, knowing and facing with purity and honesty our dependence upon the Guru for liberation. A little child lets the need for the mother be known. A little child has a boo-boo and brings it to the mother to be kissed. The mother knows, even if the child doesn't say I love you, how much the child needs her. The mother knows. It's a natural communication that they have. When the child says to the mother with total confidence, "I am hungry," the mother knows. There are no spoken words of love there, but the mother knows that the child is utterly and completely dependent. The mother knows that the child sees the mother as a fountain of blessing. The mother knows that the child's life would be lost without her support. She knows that love. When the child is cold, the child goes to the mother and asks to be held, warmed up. When the child is lonely and afraid, the child goes to the mother and asks to be rocked, loved, and sung to. Even though the child may not say, "I love you," still the mother sees the child's need and understands the relationship.

If that is so with ordinary mothers and children, then if we express our need for the Guru, without shame, or pride, or fear of being humble—God forbid we should be humble!—constantly expressing our need, our appreciation, and our confidence in the Guru, then in that way we are also expressing that we wish the Guru to remain. If our hearts are hard and we say, "Oh, nice teaching. Now I'll go and do what I need to do," and there is no relationship of that intimate nature, like a mother and a child, then there is no practice. Here's the question: Is the love so strong in your heart, is the understanding so profound and so wise, that in fact you really do wish the Buddhas to remain in the world? The way I've just given you to hold your mind and hold yourself would be the answer to that. Think of yourself as a child and the Guru as your dear, dear mother who gives you everything. We bring all our boo-boos, our coldness, our loneliness, our fear, our hunger, our hurt, everything. These things we bring, because in the face of the primordial empty nature, in the face of luminosity, in the face of the great miraculous Bodhicitta, these things disappear, and all our boo-boos are kissed.

Dedication

*By paying homage, making offerings, confession and
Rejoicing, requesting and beseeching—
Whatever virtue I have gained through these efforts,
I dedicate it all to the enlightenment of all beings!*

Dedication

'Dedication of merit can be understood as repaying the kindness of the Lama.'

The next posture that we should remain in constantly is that of returning the favor of the Guru's kindness. What kind of kindness would cause the Buddhas to appear in the world for the sake of sentient beings, experiencing all the worldly and ordinary conditions, rather than remaining constantly in the bliss of nirvana? Amazing and wonderful, isn't it? What kind of kindness would that take? The Bodhisattvas remain poised on the brink of realization—seemingly forever—emanating constantly and endlessly into the world until samsara is empty.

What kind of love would that take? We think about the love it takes for a mother to suffer and bear her young. We think of the love it takes for a mother to feed and care for her young. We think of the love it takes for a mother to patiently explain, patiently teach, and patiently go through what needs to be gone through. We're talking about the ideal mother, who would patiently explain, because all the mother would care about is raising the child so that it is fully functional, fully competent, fully happy, fully blossomed in every conceivable way.

That's a lot of love, isn't it? That's a lot of love! Just think what kind of love it would take for a loving parent to give in that way. Hardly any of us can imagine such a thing. Although the kindness of our samsaric parents is evident because we are here, many of them have not known how to love. They simply haven't known how. Their love was never perfect.

We're talking about a perfect mother. What kind of love would that be? It is practically unimaginable. If you can imagine that, how much more would it take to imagine the kind of love and compassion that it takes for the Buddhas and Bodhisattvas to appear in the world for the sake of sentient beings under ordinary conditions? Again, and again, and again. Uncountable times. What kind of love is that? We who give and take love like we change our underwear—we who give and take love according to what's in it for us—we can't even understand that.

Yet we must try. We must try to understand that level of compassion. Not only do they return for our sake, but they practice for our sake. These Buddhas and Bodhisattvas have accomplished supreme realization—many under terrible conditions, going through terrible tests and trials, which are part and parcel with their coming into their own. They've crossed this ocean of suffering under extreme effort. Lifetime after lifetime of practice and accomplishment. They did so for the sake of those who have hope of them. Having accomplished that, they return again and again and again for the sake of sentient beings, and would return for even one. What kind of love is that? What kind of compassion is that?

We should contemplate and meditate on that. Then we should think that we must repay that kindness. In order to repay that kindness, we have to think: What is the goal of the Lama? Why does the Lama appear in the world? The answer is: for the sake of sentient beings. The Lama appears in the world because it is unthinkable that sentient beings should continue to wander helplessly in samsara.

Therefore, we call on the merit that we have accomplished

in the three times, past, present, and future. We constantly look for ways to accomplish merit, constantly look for meritorious activities so that we can offer that merit for the liberation and salvation of all sentient beings. We should never, ever think, "Oh that was good. Got some!" because that's not how the Lama thinks, and we are wishing to repay the kindness of the Lama.

Dedication of merit can be understood as repaying the kindness of the Lama. The Lama has given the nectar to you. You must in turn find a way to give the nectar to the Lama, to the same degree that the Lama has done. We're not talking sloppy. That doesn't mean, "Oh, the Lama has given me the nectar, so I'll practice and I'll dedicate the merit. Period." Doesn't that thud a little when it hits the floor? We are talking about going through the same extraordinary activity that the Lama has gone through in order to accomplish their practice—achieving supreme realization, and then returning for the sake of sentient beings. This you must do in order to repay the kindness of the Guru. This is the ultimate dedication of all merit to the liberation and salvation of all sentient beings—the gathering together of extraordinary merit, the accomplishment of meritorious activity, and the returning for the sake of sentient beings. You offer that merit as a gift, as a feast, just as you have been offered the feast of Dharma by the Lama.

* * *

'Following in the footsteps of my Guru
I will accomplish.'

Instead of the feast we have offered to the Lama so far, that lovely feast of hatred, greed, ignorance, jealousy and pride, now we pay homage. We make offerings, we offer confession. We rejoice in the capacity of those who have accomplished. We request the nectar of the teachings. We beseech the Lama, the Buddhas, and the Bodhisattvas to remain in the world for the sake of sentient beings. We pay back the great kindness of the Guru by dedicating all the merit that we have ever accomplished, or will ever accomplish in the three times, for the liberation and salvation of all sentient beings. We make the commitment here and now—right this moment—that we ourselves will not rest until we achieve supreme realization so that we can return for the sake of sentient beings. Following in the footsteps of my Guru, I will accomplish. This is the prayer. This is how we practice.

I request that you go through this teaching making notes, because there are pointing-out instructions here that I consider concentrated, important and many-layered. If you really comb through it in a responsible way, extracting from it every single bit of nectar that you can, you will receive a lot more.

Please accomplish the practice in that way and think that this is how you should be from this moment forward. Inside, this is your practice. You need not look any different at all on the outside. In fact, it would be best if you didn't! Because I would say that it was an act. There doesn't have to be any words, there doesn't have to be any show. It should begin within you, quietly, in a deep and profound way, indicating that at last you have entered into the well of your own natural mind, and have begun to draw up the nectar, the nectar of the Guru.

ཨར་ལག་བདུན་པ་ནི།

The Seven Branch Offering[2]
[also referred to as the Seven Limb Puja]

Visualize all the Buddhas, Bodhisattvas and masters in front of you

འཕགས་པ་བཟང་པོ་སྤྱོད་པའི་སྨོན་ལམ་གྱི་རྒྱལ་པོ།

PHAGPA ZANG PO CHOD PE MONLAM GYI GYAL PO
The King of Noble Prayers aspiring to the deeds of the Excellent

འཕགས་པ་འཇམ་དཔལ་གཞོན་ནུར་གྱུར་པ་ལ་ཕྱག་འཚལ་ལོ།

PHAGPA JAMPAL ZHON NUR GYUR PA LA CHAG TSAL LO
Homage to the ever-youthful Arya Manjushri!

Paying homage to the Buddhas and Bodhisattvas

ཇི་སྙེད་སུ་དག་ཕྱོགས་བཅུའི་འཇིག་རྟེན་ན།

JI NYED SU DAG CHOG CHU'I JIG TEN NA
Throughout all the worlds in the ten directions,

དུས་གསུམ་གཤེགས་པ་མི་ཡི་སེང་གེ་ཀུན།

DÜ SUM SHEG PA MI YI SENGE KÜN
Dwell the sugatas of the three times, lions among men,

བདག་གིས་མ་ལུས་དེ་དག་ཐམས་ཅད་ལ།

DAG GI MA LÜ DE DAG THAM CHED LA
To all of them without exception

---

[2] From the Gandavyuha chapter of the Avatamsaka Sutra. Source of this translation: Palyul Ling International. Namchö Daily Practice. McDonough, New York, 2010.

VIEWING THE GURU THRU THE LENS OF THE SEVEN LIMB PUJA

LÜ DANG NGAG YID DANG WE CHAG GYI-O
With devotion I bow down with my body, speech and mind.

ZANG PO JÖD PA'I MÖNLAM TOB DAG GI
By the strength of this aspiration to the deeds of the excellent,

GYALWA THAM CHED YID KYI NGÖN SUM DU
And by envisioning myself in the presence of all the victorious ones,

ZHING GI DÜL NYED LÜ RAB TÜD PA YI
Prostrating to them with bodies as numberless as the atoms of this world,

GYALWA KÜN LA RAB TU CHAG TSAL LO
I pay homage to every Buddha!

DÜL CHIG TENG NA DÜL NYED SANGYE NAM
Upon each atom are as many Buddhas as atoms exist,

SANGYE SE KYI Ü NA SHUG PA DANG
Each seated in the midst of gathered Bodhisattvas.

The Seven Limb Puja

དེ་ལྟར་ཆོས་ཀྱི་དབྱིངས་རྣམས་མ་ལུས་པ།

DE TAR CHÖ KYI YING NAM MA LÜ PA
In this way the entire Dharmadhatu excluding nothing,

མས་ཅད་རྒྱལ་བ་དག་གིས་གང་བར་མོས།

THAM CHED GYALWA DAG GI GANG WAR MÖ
Is imagined to be completely filled by victorious ones.

དེ་དག་བསྔགས་པ་མི་ཟད་རྒྱ་མཚོ་རྣམས།

DE DAG NGAG PA MI ZED GYATSHO NAM
Rendering praises inexhaustible as the ocean.

དབྱངས་ཀྱི་ཡན་ལག་རྒྱ་མཚོའི་སྒྲ་ཀུན་གྱིས།

YANG KYI YEN LAG GYATSHO'I DRA KÜN GYI
In melodious tones as boundless as the sea,

རྒྱལ་བ་ཀུན་གྱི་ཡོན་ཏན་རབ་བརྗོད་ཅིང་།

GYALWA KÜN GYI YÖN TEN RAB DZÖD CHING
The enlightened qualities of all the conquerors are acknowledged,

བདེ་བར་གཤེགས་པ་ཐམས་ཅད་བདག་གིས་བསྟོད།

DE WAR SHEGPA THAM CHED DAG GI TÖD
And I praise all Sugatas!

Making Offerings such as incense and flowers to all the Buddhas and Bodhisattvas

མེ་ཏོག་དམ་པ་ཕྲེང་བ་དམ་པ་དང་།

ME TOG DAM PA TRENG WA DAM PA DANG
Excellent garlands of mangnificent flowers,

VIEWING THE GURU THRU THE LENS OF THE SEVEN LIMB PUJA

SIL NYEN NAM DANG JUG PA DUG CHOG DANG
Instrumentation, oils and the best of parasols,

MAR ME CHOG DANG DUG PÖ DAM PA YI
Splendid butter lamps and sacred incense;

GYALWA DE DAG LA NI CHÖD PAR GYI
All of this is offered to the victorious ones (Buddhas)!.

NA ZA DAM PA NAM DANG DRI CHOG DANG
The finest of garments and superior perfumes

CHE MA PHUR MA RI RAB NYAM PA DANG
And fragrant powder equalling Sumeru,

KÖD PA KHYED PAR PHAG PA'I CHOG KÜN GYI
This magnificent array of the finest and best of them all

GYALWA DE DAG LA NI CHÖD PAR GYI
Is offered to the victorious ones (Buddhas)!

CHÖD PA GANG NAM LA MED GYA CHE WA
Whatever is offered is unsurpassed in opulence,

The Seven Limb Puja

DE DAG GYAL WA THAM CHED LA YANG MÖ
And directed with utmost devotion to all the Buddhas.

ZANG PO CHÖD LA DED PA'I TOB DAG GI
By the strength of faith of this aspiration of the deeds of excellence,

GYAL WA KÜN LA CHAG TSAL CHÖD PAR GYI
Paying homage to all the Buddhas, these offerings are made.

Confessing negative actions from desire, ignorance, anger, pride and envy in the presence of all Buddhas and Bodhisattvas

DÖD CHAG ZHE DANG TI MUG WANG GI NI
Overpowered by desire, anger and delusion,

LÜ DANG NGAG DANG DE ZHIN YID KYI KYANG
With my body, my speech and similarly with my mind,

DIG PA DAG GI GYI PA CHI CHI PA
Whatever negativity that I have amassed,

DE DAG THAM CHED DAG GI SO SOR SHAG
I confess individually and entirely.

Viewing the Guru Thru the Lens of the Seven Limb Puja

Rejoicing in the merit of all sentient beings, Buddhas and Bodhisattvas.

ཕྱོགས་བཅུའི་རྒྱལ་བ་ཀུན་དང་སངས་རྒྱས་སྲས།

CHOG CHU'I GYAL WA KÜN DANG SANGYE SE
The merit of all the victorious ones of the ten directions and their heirs,

རང་རྒྱལ་རྣམས་དང་སློབ་དང་མི་སློབ་དང་།

RANG GYAL NAM DANG LOB DANG MI LOB DANG
Of the solitary realizers and those on the paths of learning and no more learning,

འགྲོ་བ་ཀུན་གྱི་བསོད་ནམས་གང་ལ་ཡང་།

DRO WA KÜN GYI SÖD NAM GANG LA YANG
And of every sentient being without exception -- ,

དེ་དག་ཀུན་གྱི་རྗེས་སུ་བདག་ཡི་རང་།

DE DAG KÜN GYI JE SU DAG YI RANG
I fully rejoice in all such accumulations!

Requesting that the wheel of Dharma be turned

གང་རྣམས་ཕྱོགས་བཅུའི་འཇིག་རྟེན་སྒྲོན་མ་རྣམས།

GANG NAM CHOG CHU'I JIG TEN DRÖN MA NAM
All those who illuminate the world systems of the ten directions,

བྱང་ཆུབ་རིམ་པར་སངས་རྒྱས་མ་ཆགས་བརྙེས།

CHANG CHUB RIM PAR SANGYE MA CHAG NYE
Who have attained buddhahood and freedom from attachment through the stages of enlightenment,,

The Seven Limb Puja

མགོན་པོ་དེ་དག་བདག་གིས་ཐམས་ཅད་ལ།
GÖN PO DE DAG DAG GI THAM CHED LA
I implore all those protectors

འཁོར་ལོ་བླ་ན་མེད་པར་བསྐོར་བར་བསྐུལ།
KHOR LO LA NA MED PAR KOR WAR KUL
To turn the peerless wheel of the Dharma!

Requesting the Buddhas and Bodhisattvas not to enter Nirvana

མྱ་ངན་འདའ་སྟོན་གང་བཞེད་དེ་དག་ལ།
NYA NGEN DA TÖN GANG ZHED DE DAG LA
All you who intend to display entering nirvana,

འགྲོ་བ་ཀུན་ལ་ཕན་ཞིང་བདེ་བའི་ཕྱིར།
DRO WA KÜN LA PHEN ZHING DE WA'I CHIR
For the purpose of bringing benefit and bliss to all beings,

བསྐལ་པ་ཞིང་གི་རྡུལ་སྙེད་བཞུགས་པར་ཡང་།
KALPA ZHING KI DÜL NYED ZHUG PAR YANG
For as many eons as there are particles of dust on earth,.

བདག་གིས་ཐལ་མོ་རབ་སྦྱར་གསོལ་བར་བགྱི།
DAG GI THAL MO RAB CHAR SÖL WAR GYI
With palms pressed together I beseech you to remain in the world!

Dedicatng the merit

ཕྱག་འཚལ་བ་དང་མཆོད་ཅིང་བཤགས་པ་དང་།
CHAG TSAL WA DANG CHÖD CHING SHAG PA DANG
By paying homage, making offerings, confession and

རྗེས་སུ་ཡིད་རང་བསྐུལ་ཞིང་གསོལ་བ་ཡི།

JE SU YID RANG KÜL ZHING SÖLWA YI
Rejoicing, requesting and beseeching --

དགེ་བ་ཆུང་ཟད་བདག་གིས་ཅི་བསགས་པ།

GE WA CHUNG ZED DAG GI CHI SAG PA
Whatever virtue I have gained through these efforts,

ཐམས་ཅད་བདག་གིས་བྱང་ཆུབ་ཕྱིར་བསྔོའོ།

THAM CHED DAG GI CHANG CHUB CHIR NGO WO
I dedicate it all to the enlightenment of all beings!

GLOSSARY

Awake/Awakened: A term used interchangeably for enlightenment. (See also 'Buddha' and 'Enlightened' in this Glossary.)

Bodhicitta: The mind of enlightenment that encompasses wisdom and compassion.

Bodhisattva: One who embodies Bodhicitta. A Bodhisattva vows to rescue all beings from their suffering and guide them to enlightenment.

Buddha: The historical founder of Buddhism, Shakyamuni. Also, one who is completely awake to his or her true nature and the true nature of all reality.

Buddhist: One who, from the depths of their heart, has taken refuge in the Three Precious Jewels of Buddhism—the Buddha, Dharma, and Sangha. (See also 'Refuge' in this Glossary.)

Compassion: Activity motivated by concern for others. (See also Practical Compassion/Bodhicitta and Aspirational Compassion/Bodhicitta in this Glossary.)

Dakini: Primordial wisdom in female form, an enlightened female.

Dharma: The pure path taught by the Buddha that leads one out of suffering into the awakened state of enlightenment. Dharma is the underlying meaning of the Buddha's teachings; the truth upon which all Buddhist practices, scriptures, and philosophy are founded.

Dharmadhatu: The 'realm of phenomena'; the suchness in which emptiness and dependent origination are inseparable. (See 'Suchness' and 'Primordial' in this Glossary.)

Emptiness: The complete absence of true existence in all phenomena.

Enlightenment: Enlightenment is the cessation of suffering, reached when the qualities of compassion and wisdom are perfected, and all non-virtue has been extinguished from one's mind.

Guru: One's spiritual teacher.

Guru Yoga: The disciplined practice of mixing one's mind with the mind of the teacher.

Ignorance: One of the main causes of suffering along with hatred and greed; a lack of awareness of cause and effect relationships.

Incarnation: The form one takes lifetime after lifetime in any one of the six realms. (See also 'Cyclic Existence' in this Glossary.)

Karma: Universal law of cause and effect governing the activity of unenlightened beings, whereby all experience is the result or fruit of some previous action or cause. Through the force of intention we perform actions with our body, speech, and mind, and all of these actions produce effects. The effect of virtuous actions is happiness and the effect of negative actions is suffering.

Lama: Also means one's spiritual teacher, often used interchangeably with Guru.

Mandala: A physical or visual display of enlightened activity.

Meditation: Encompasses various forms of mind practice to increase spiritual awareness. There are two principal forms of meditation practice: the development of concentration and the development of insight.

Meditational deities: Enlightened representations in male, female, peaceful and wrathful form which are the source of spiritual accomplishment.

Practice: Any activity that moves one closer to the goal of Enlightenment. This can include meditation, contemplation, mantra recitation and prayer.

Pratyekabuddha: Someone who attains a level of realization without the help of a spiritual master.

Primordial: The fundamental, natural state; the ground of being.

Refuge: In the Buddhist context, the objects that protect us from suffering, e.g., the Buddha, the Buddha's teachings and the community of practitioners.

Root Guru: The teacher who first exposes one to their true nature.

Samadhi: A state of meditative absorption.

Samsara: The endless round of death and rebirth, characterized by impermanence, cause and effect, suffering, and ignorance of true reality. (See also 'Karma' and 'Ignorance' in this Glossary).

Sangha: The community of Buddhist monks and nuns; may also refer to lay practitioners.

Self-nature: Ego structure.

Sentient Being: A sentient being is any living being that experiences feelings through their senses, and also refers to a being who has not yet reached enlightenment.

Sugata: A Buddha

Tathagata: A Buddha.

Vajrayana: One of the three vehicles of Buddhism that also contains the other vehicles—Theravada and Mahayana within it. Vajrayana, otherwise known as the "Diamond Vehicle," is practiced mostly by Buddhists following the Tibetan, Mongolian and Himalayan forms of Buddhism.

View: The understanding that from the perspective of enlightened perception, there is no self and other, no subject and object. All phenomenal reality is inseparable and nondual.

Dedication

By this effort may all sentient beings
be free of suffering.

May their minds be filled with the
nectar of virtue.

In this way may all causes resulting in suffering
be extinguished,

And only the light of compassion
shine throughout all realms.

—*Jetsunma Ahkön Norbu Lhamo*

To read more of Jetsunma's teachings
visit her blog
Tibetan Buddhist Altar
www.tibetanbuddhistaltar.org

About Jetsunma Ahkön Lhamo

From an early age, Jetsunma Ahkön Norbu Lhamo has devoted herself to meditation and the alleviation of suffering in the world. With confirmation from two highly revered Tibetan Buddhist masters, His Holiness Dilgo Khyentse Rinpoche and Dzongnang Rinpoche, His Holiness Penor Rinpoche, 11th throneholder of the Palyul Lineage in the Nyingma tradition, recognized Jetsunma as a reincarntion of the 17th century yogini Genyenma Ahkön Lhamo. The first Ahkön Lhamo was the sister of Rigdzin Kunzang Sherab, the founder and first Throneholder of Palyul.

Subsequently, His Holiness Kusum Lingpa recognized Jetsunma as an emanation of Princess Lhacham Mandarava, the Indian consort of Padmasambhava (also known as Guru Rinpoche, or Precious Teacher), the Indian scholar who established Buddhism in Tibet. Jetsunma is the first Western woman to have been officially recognized and enthroned as a Tulku, an enlightened being who reincarnates in whatever form necessary to benefit sentient beings.

With innate compassion and wisdom, and drawing on her experiences as a Western woman, Jetsunma makes even the most profound Buddhist teachings accessible. Her teachings, often infused with humor, reach a broad audience, including long-time Buddhist practitioners as well as people simply wanting to live with kindness and generosity. Jetsunma encourages each of us to create a world of compassion, by contemplating the suffering of others, and taking action to bring about change.

Jetsunma Ahkön Lhamo gives an inspiring and down-to-earth interpretation of the key aspects of devotion and the proper way of viewing an authentic spiritual guide. Through the lens of the Tibetan Buddhist practice—the Seven Limb Puja—Jetsunma brings to light the essential aspects of Guru Yoga for the Western mind.